READ WHAT CAN HAPPEN WHEN YOU
Never Give Up and Go For It!

LETTERS FROM AMERICAN HEROES
ANDY ANDREWS, AUTHOR OF *STORMS OF PERFECTION*

Dedicated to Meg (age 13), Max (age 12), and Collin Reed (age 3),
Tristan (age 16), Maggie (age 13) and Sara Grace McClain (age 10)
— you will be in a book like this one day!
Special thanks to Ben and Jackie Peters for introducing me to Dalmatian Press.

This children's book series is based on the
Andy Andrews book series *Storms of Perfection*.™

Publisher, Producer: Chris Hilicki
Cover Illustration: Kevin Menck, Text Illustrations: Jerry Dillingham
Art Direction: Andy Mangrum, Photos of Andy Andrews: Peter Nash

ALL ART AND EDITORIAL MATERIAL OWNED BY DALMATIAN PRESS, LLC.
ISBN: 1-57759-778-8
First Published in the United States in 2002 by Dalmatian Press, LLC.
Copyright©2002 Dalmatian Press, LLC. Printed and bound in Canada.
The DALMATIAN PRESS name and logo are
trademarks of Dalmatian Press, Franklin, Tennessee 37067.

All rights reserved. Written permission must be secured from
the publisher to use or reproduce any part of this book,
except for brief quotations in critical reviews or publicity.
11856
02 03 04 QWB 10 9 8 7 6 5 4 3 2 1

Table of Contents

U.S. Army General
General Norman Schwarzkopf 1

Fire Chief
Fire Chief James Lesnick 5

Vietnam Veteran
Clebe McClary 9

Congresswoman
Congresswoman Sue Myrick 13

WWII Prisoner of War
John F. Northcott 17

Astronaut
Captain Walter Schirra 21

FBI Director
William S. Sessions 25

Astronaut
Admiral Alan Shepard 29

U.S. Army General
General William Westmoreland 33

Test Pilot & U.S. Air Force General
General Chuck Yeager 37

Andy Andrews 40
Journal Pages 43

H. Norman Schwarzkopf

U.S. Army General

★ ★ ★ ★

Have you heard of a four-star general? A star is a medal you earn from the Army for being brave and smart. Very few people have been able to get four stars. One of those people is General Norman Schwarzkopf.

He helped America fight in a country called Vietnam. He also led the attack against the country of Iraq. This was called the Persian Gulf War. It was also called Operation Desert Storm. It took place in a desert far away.

He has had many good things happen to him in his life. But there were times when people didn't believe in him. There were times when people said, "YOU AREN'T THE RIGHT MAN FOR THE JOB." But he learned important lessons from those times. He learned about patience. He learned to be understanding. And he learned to always focus on the positive things.

HOW MANY STARS WILL YOU EARN IN LIFE? GO FOR IT!

In Their Own Words

Dear Andy,

When I received your invitation to share a time of discouragement in my life, my concern was how to select only one.

In 1974, two events happened. First, the Army released its list for early promotion. I'd not been selected. A few days later, I was told I had not been selected to work with Gerald Ford. My frustration level was at an all time high.

I must tell you two of the most important lessons I learned from those challenges. (1) Don't dwell on disappointment—do your best anyway. And (2) we don't always know what's best.

Looking back at my career, I can see now that every struggle pointed me toward my destiny in the Gulf War. We don't always know what's best. The tough times in my life often dealt with being put in positions not of my choosing. But the result is now a matter of history.

Success without adversity is not only empty… it is not possible.

Sincerely,

H. Norman Schwarzkopf
General, U.S. Army, Retired

Fire Chief

James Lesnick

★ ★ ★ ★

Have you ever watched a fire in a fireplace?

Small fires can be helpful. They can even be pretty.

But when fires are bigger, they can be dangerous.

A fireman is the brave person who fights fires. He helps protect our homes and families.

Jim Lesnick knew he wanted to be a firefighter when he grew up. He wanted to help people. He helped out at his local fire department. He learned about fire safety. He talked to lots of people about how to prevent fires. He told them, **"I WILL TEACH YOU HOW TO BE SAFE."** He talked to schools, churches, and clubs. After high school, he studied Fire Protection at college. Soon, he was a real firefighter!

He started collecting firefighter stuff like hats and badges when he was only four years old. He even has his own fire truck! Now he has one of the biggest private collections in America. People visit his museum all the time to learn about firemen and how they save lives.

DO YOU LIKE TO HELP PEOPLE?
CAN YOU HELP TO MAKE YOUR
TOWN A SAFER PLACE?
GO FOR IT!

In Their Own Words

Dear Andy,

All of my life I have wanted to be a firefighter. When I was four years old I hung out at the firehouse. My uncle was a fireman there. I loved the excitement of the sirens and trucks. I loved the "heroes" coming to save people.

I knew becoming a firefighter was the right thing. When we go on an alarm, we are helping someone who needs us. Firefighters are like a family. That makes my job very special.

Most times firefighters can make things right. But sometimes they can't – the fire is too big. Even then, firefighters can't stop trying to help. They know that in times like this the people they serve truly need them the most. It is a hard job. But every time the alarm rings they fight a fire again.

A firefighter's job is a lot like problems you will face in your life. You have to face your problem, no matter how hard it is. You have to deal with it and not let it beat you. Always do your best. In the end you will feel good about what you have been able to do.

When the Pentagon was attacked in September 2001, I went to Washington, D.C. to help fight the fires. I was thankful for all my training and experiences. They prepared me for this terrible thing that happened. Now and always I am proud to protect people, our homes, and our great country.

Sincerely,

James E. Lesnick

James Lesnick

Clebe McClary

Vietnam Veteran

Do you know what a Purple Heart is? It is a medal given to soldiers who have been hurt during a war. Clebe McClary has three Purple Hearts. He lost his eye and his arm fighting for our country. And even badly hurt, he still saved the lives of 8 men!

Some people might say, "HOW CAN HE HAVE A POSITIVE ATTITUDE? SO MANY BAD THINGS HAVE HAPPENED TO HIM!" Mr. McClary's wife is named Deanna. She was with him almost every day as he got well. She would feed him and pray with him. She wrote a book about that time. It is called "Commitment To Love."

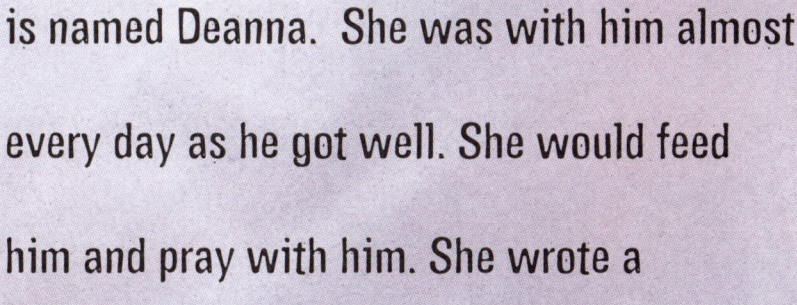

Everyone talks about how brave Clebe McClary was. He was wounded seven times in Vietnam.

He had 34 operations. He was in the hospital for 2 years. The President of the United States said that he was a hero. The President gave him two more medals. They are called the Bronze Star and the Silver Star.

HOW MANY MEDALS
WILL YOU EARN IN YOU LIFE?
GO FOR IT!

In Their Own Words

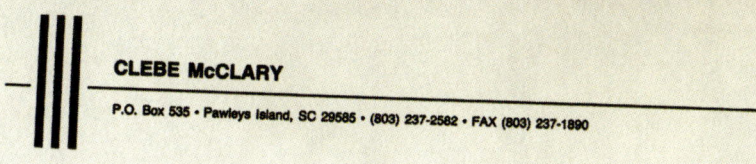

CLEBE McCLARY
P.O. Box 535 • Pawleys Island, SC 29585 • (803) 237-2582 • FAX (803) 237-1890

Dear Andy,

I spent 2 1/2 years in the hospital and 34 major operations, after being wounded seven times in Vietnam.

Deanna, my wife, gave me a reason to live. She has stood by me for 26 years. The storms we've had in our lives have made us a stronger couple.

We realize that changes come in everyone's life. Mine were visibly physical, with the loss of an arm and an eye.

Several acronyms I use to weather the storms in life are:
PATCH, because I wear one on my eye. It reminds me that it is a Positive Attitude That Creates Hope.
BIONIC: Believe It Or Not, I Care. I think we need to care about others.
FIDO has become my motto. It's the license tag on my car. Forget It and Drive On. Forget about your problems. Don't dwell on them. Good experience, bad experience, just learn from it and get on with your life.

I appreciate what you're doing, Andy. The rest of your life will be the best of your life because you are investing in the lives of others!

In His Grip,

Clebe & Deanna McClary

Sue Myrick

Congress-woman

★ ★ ★ ★

For many years, Sue Myrick was a great wife and mom. She was very happy. She lived in Charlotte, North Carolina. But she said to herself,

"THE LOCAL GOVERNMENT SHOULD HELP FAMILIES MORE."

Most people would only complain. They would want other people to fix the problems. Not Sue Myrick. She ran for mayor! She was the mayor for eight years. She led the fight against drugs. She made taxes lower. She helped bring the Carolina Panthers football team to her city.

In 1994, she was elected to Congress. She has an office in Washington, D.C. She works hard to  make our country better. It was just a few years ago that she decided to help others. Now she helps people every day. And now and then she gets to eat lunch with the President!

WHO DO YOU WANT TO HELP?
WOULD YOU LIKE TO EAT LUNCH WITH THE PRESIDENT?
GO FOR IT!

In Their Own Words

Congress of the United States
House of Representatives
Washington, DC 20515

Dear Andy,

There is an old saying that goes, "the world will never meet you half way." I have found this to be true. Overcoming obstacles is an experience all people will go through if they want success.

From December of 1991 through May of 1992, I ran for the United States Senate. I ran a common-sense campaign. I toured the state and met with voters.

This campaign was marked by name-calling. My opponent's accusations appeared on television. Strapped for cash, I was unable to respond.

I finished second in the race. People thought my career was over. But in 1994, I was elected to the United States House of Representatives.

I know today that I am a stronger person because of the Senate race. I had run a race of "integrity." I learned that winning or losing is not defined by the final vote.

Sincerely,

Sue Myrick
Member of Congress

John Northcott

WWII POW

John Northcott was just a young man in 1941. He worked on a boat in the Navy. Then World War II started. He and his shipmates fought in places that are now famous. He was at a place called Bataan with General Douglas MacArthur.

Later that year, he was caught by the enemy on an island called Corregidor. He was a prisoner of war (POW) for almost four years. A lot of the time he did not have food or water. A lot of his friends became sick. They could not get any medicine. But Mr. Northcott kept a good attitude. He tried to make his friends feel better when he could.

At one point, he was sent to a factory to work. When he was rescued, he was very happy! Today, he is still happy. He doesn't let little things bother him or get him down. He says, "I AM THANKFUL TO HAVE ENOUGH TO EAT. I AM GRATEFUL FOR MY WARM BED!"

WHAT CAN YOU FIND TO BE HAPPY ABOUT TODAY? GO FOR IT!

In Their Own Words

JOHN F. NORTHCOTT
805 Oak Drive
Leesburg, Florida 34748-4322

Dear Andy,

It was not difficult to choose the toughest storm in my life. It was December 7, 1941. The Japanese had attacked Pearl Harbor.

We were ordered to report to Corregidor. Corregidor was being bombed everyday. On May 10, our officers told us Corregidor had surrendered. The surrender point was an area of concrete. We stayed in this place for three weeks. They did not feed us.

A condemned prison was where we got our first solid meal—watery boiled rice. We boarded the ship to Japan. We ate a couple of tablespoons of raw rice every 2 or 3 days. 42 days later, we reached Japan. When we were liberated, I weighed 65 pounds, but considered myself lucky. Of the 30,000 of us who had been captured 43 months earlier, only 3,000 of us survived.

People might find it impossible to believe that anything positive could have come out of these experiences. But the storm has given me a gratefulness of little things that others do not have.

I watch people who let a headache ruin their day. Financial troubles and cancelled flights give people high blood pressure. But to me, those things are no big deal. I'm just happy to be here!

Sincerely,
John F. Northcott
John F. Northcott
U.S.N. Retired

Walter M. Schirra

Astronaut

NASA picked seven men to be the first astronauts. Wally Schirra was one of them. The first time he went into space was in the space capsule called Mercury. He went around the earth six times. He was traveling at 17,557 miles per hour. That's **really** over the speed limit!

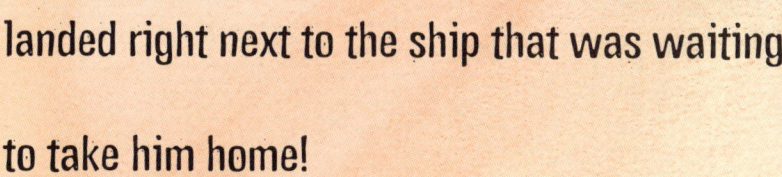

He took his second flight on Gemini VI. His third trip into space was also his last. It was on Apollo VII. The flight lasted for 11 days. He traveled more than 5 million miles. When he got back to earth, he landed right next to the ship that was waiting to take him home!

Now he speaks to large groups of people.

He asks them to learn more about outer space.

He says, "THERE ARE MANY THINGS LEFT FOR US TO LEARN. THERE ARE LOTS OF PLACES LEFT TO EXPLORE."

WOULD YOU LIKE TO EXPLORE ANOTHER PLANET? HOW WOULD YOU LIKE TO FLY A ROCKET TO THE MOON? GO FOR IT!

In Their Own Words

Walter M. Schirra
16834 Via de Santa Fe, Box 73
Rancho Santa Fe, CA 92067

Dear Andy,

My first venture into space was on 3 October 1962. Three years later, Tom Stafford and I went to man Gemini 6 for a launch. We went through countdown and waited for confirmation that the Agena, our target for the world's first rendezvous, was in orbit.

No joy! The Agena failed to orbit. Three years of training down the drain!

Fortunately, we could launch after Gemini 7 and use them for our target. On 12 December 1965, Tom and I went through another smooth countdown. But we did not lift off. A milli-second decision by me solved a tough problem. The engines did start, then shut down. If we had lifted off a massive explosion would occur on shutdown. We could have ejected to safety. Or we could sit it out, as we did.

On 15 December 1965 Tom and I went through a third countdown. We accomplished the world's first rendezvous with Gemini 7.

Three times, a charm, proved to us the logic about keep trying when the going gets tough.

Sincerely yours,

Wally Schirra
Mercury 8
Gemini 6
Apollo 7

William S. Sessions

FBI Director

Have you heard of the FBI's "Ten Most Wanted" list? William Sessions was once the Director of the FBI. He was in charge of all the FBI agents in America. His job was to keep the United States safe for all of us.

For many years, he worked as a lawyer in Texas. He left there to go work with the Department of Justice in Washington. Later, he became a judge. And then the President called him. He said, "I WOULD LIKE YOU TO RUN THE FBI!"

Many good things happened while he was in charge. The FBI captured bank robbers, drug dealers, and crooks of all kinds.

WOULD YOU LIKE TO BE AN FBI AGENT ONE DAY? WOULD YOU LIKE TO HELP KEEP AMERICA SAFE? GO FOR IT!

In Their Own Words

U.S. Department of Justice

Federal Bureau of Investigation

Office of the Director

Washington, D.C. 20535

Dear Andy,

One event had more impact on my life than any other. As a 16-year-old, I contracted polio. My right shoulder, arm, and hand became useless. An appointment was made for me at St. Marys Hospital to begin my treatment.

The next morning, I walked through the doors to the center. What confronted me stopped me in my tracks. I saw iron lung machines filled with young people for whom the machines were "breathing." Other young people were struggling on parallel bars, padded stairways and other contraptions.

I burst into tears and left the room. Suddenly all of the bitterness and anger that had been welled up in me were washed away, and was replaced by gratitude for what God had spared me.

That gratitude remains with me to this day. Not a day goes by but I am reminded of how fortunate I am. All of us have a responsibility to be sensitive to others.

Sincerely,

William S. Sessions
Director

Alan Shepard

Astronaut

★ ★ ★ ★

Have you ever thought of flying into outer space? What if you could float around the room and do 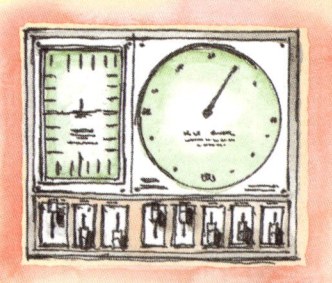 a handstand on a chair or a double back flip? Alan Shepard was the first man ever to do just that! He was the first man in space.

When Alan Shepard left earth in the rocket, he was scared. No one was sure if he would safely return, but he did. He was a hero to many people. He was on TV. He was in magazines. There were even parades held in his honor.

There was a time when he got very sick. Some 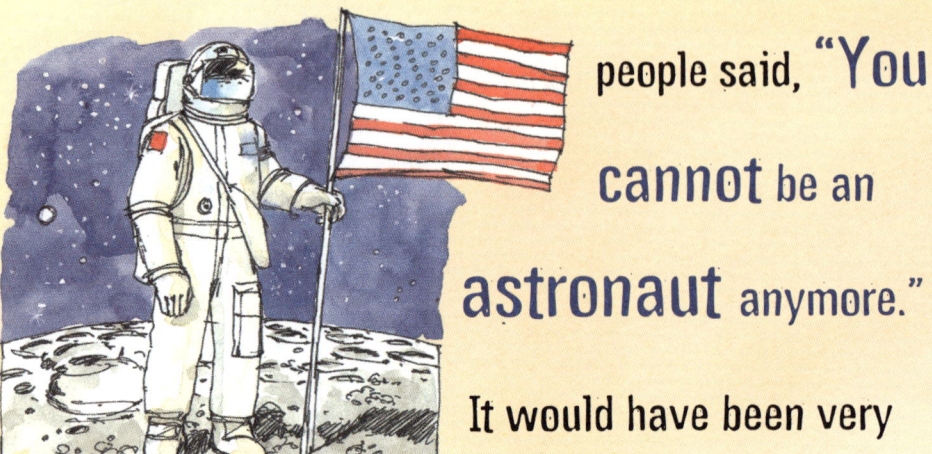 people said, "You cannot be an astronaut anymore." It would have been very easy for him to quit, but he did not. A doctor helped him with an operation. Soon he was well. The very next year, Alan Shepard actually walked on the moon!

HOW HIGH WILL YOU SET YOUR SIGHTS? CAN YOU SHOOT FOR THE MOON? GO FOR IT!

In Their Own Words

SEVEN FOURTEEN ENTERPRISES INC.

Admiral Alan Shepard
President

Dear Andy:

Perhaps the most disappointing setback of my life occurred when I was at the "peak" of my career as an astronaut.

In 1963 NASA assigned me to command the first two-man Gemini spacecraft. I was on top of the world. We were a couple of months into training when it happened! I got out of bed with loss of balance, nausea and ringing in my left ear.

NASA grounded me and told me I could stick around in a desk job. I was devastated. I tried to adjust, but became totally frustrated. I thought of quitting. But then I thought that I must not give up! I trained and kept ready.

One day I heard of a doctor who might be able to correct my problem with surgery. He decided that an operation might help. I had the operation. Then came a long recuperative period, but I didn't give up. Almost a year after the operation NASA said I could fly!

I was selected then to command Apollo 14, the third moon landing. I became the fifth man to walk on the moon! What a great personal victory that was! Had I not believed in myself, it might never have happened!

My best wishes,

Alan Shepard

Alan B. Shepard, Jr.
Rear Admiral, USN (retired)

William Westmoreland

U.S. Army General

★ ★ ★ ★

What do you think it would be like to have your picture on a magazine? General William Westmoreland was once on the cover of "TIME" magazine. He was named their "Man of the Year."

A long time ago, we were at war in a place called Vietnam. For four years, the General was the leader of all the US forces who were fighting there. As the leader, he felt a lot of pressure to do the right thing. Some people agreed with his choices. Some did not. He was on the evening news a lot. He was in the newspapers every day! He worked hard to do what he felt was right.

The General served our country for many years. He is retired now. But he says, "I AM PROUD OF DOING MY DUTY FOR THE UNITED STATES." We read about him now in history books.

HOW CAN YOU SERVE OUR COUNTRY? WOULD YOU LIKE TO READ ABOUT YOURSELF IN A HISTORY BOOK? GO FOR IT!

In Their Own Words

```
William Childs Westmoreland
General, United States Army, Retired
            Box 1059
   Charleston, South Carolina  29402
```

Dear Andy,

Many Americans saw action in World War II and Korea. Soldiers of my vintage had South Vietnam.

Wars are all different. But all have similarities. People are killed and wounded by weapons manned by people.

My first assignment was with a unit armed with weapons drawn by teams of six horses. Some 26 years later, I found myself fighting an unpopular war in Southeast Asia.

It was my privilege to command those fine young Americans in that conflict.

Every generation has its challenges. Americans of the 1960's and 70's had a heavy load. They did their best. They played a major role in making our World safe.

Sincerely,

William C. Westmoreland

William C. Westmoreland

Chuck Yeager

Test Pilot & U.S. Air Force General

When your best friend yells your name from across the playground, it just takes an instant for the sound of his voice to reach your ears. The time it takes is called the speed of sound. People said, "NO ONE WILL EVER FLY IN AN AIRPLANE AS FAST AS THE SPEED OF SOUND."

But General Chuck Yeager was the first man to fly a jet that fast! He is a very brave man. He has flown over 183 different types of airplanes in his life. Many people say that he is a legend. There was a book written about his life. Then he flew another jet that went **twice** the speed of sound. There was even a movie made about him. It was called "The Right Stuff."

He was a hero in World War II. This was when he was a very young man. He was very brave. He helped someone who was hurt, and the President of the United States gave him a medal.

HOW FAST WILL YOU FLY IN YOUR LIFE? GO FOR IT!

In Their Own Words

YEAGER, INC.
P.O. Box 128
Cedar Ridge, CA 95924
(916) 273-8681

Dear Andy:

The question I'm asked most often is whether I think I have "the right stuff." The question always annoys me because it implies that a guy with the right stuff was born that way. Experience is everything.

One of the secrets of my success has always been facing problems head on. During World War II, I faced one of the toughest challenges of my life.

I had been shot down over Nazi Germany on March 5, 1944. I made contact with members of the French Underground. We were told we would have to cross the mountains alone to reach Spain. We were up to our knees in snow. At first we would rest every hour, then every half-hour, then every fifteen minutes.

I saw the thin line of a road that I figured must be Spain. I hiked another twenty miles to the nearest village. I slept for two days. It was March 30, 1944.

As I became the first man to fly faster than the speed of sound, I remembered how I beat the first mountains in my life. I never quit... even when the evidence indicated that I should!

Sincerely,

Chuck

Charles E. Yeager
Brig. Gen., USAF, Ret.

Andy Andrews

Andy Andrews has been inspiring people for over two decades. He is an author, entertainer, speaker, and comedian. He has spoken to millions of people—including four Presidents of the United States!

Dear Friend,

I found out early in my life that if you don't give up hope, good news is right around the corner! Sometimes, bad things happen to good people. As you can see by the letters in this book, successful people have problems, too.

One difference between successful people and everyone else is that the successful people never seem to quit. Even when times are tough, they smile and keep going. That is why they have become people we admire. Successful people have great attitudes—just like you!

Won't it be terrific to grow up and see yourself in a book like this? I CAN'T WAIT TO READ YOUR STORY! GO FOR IT!

Your friend

Andy Andrews

In Your Own Words

Do you have your own story about how you **NEVER GAVE UP** you'd like to share with Andy? Use this letter to tell Andy how you've learned to keep trying, to believe in your dreams, and to never give up. Maybe you'll spot your letter in one of Andy's future books!

Dear Andy,

_____

_____

_____

_____

_____

_____

_____

_____

Ask an adult to help you cut out this letter. Put your letter in an addressed, stamped envelope and send it to: Andy Andrews, Never Give Up and Go For It, PO Box 17321, Nashville, TN, 37217 or go to: www.AndyAndrews.com.

WHAT IS ONE OF THE THINGS YOU'D LIKE TO DO WHEN YOU GROW UP?

_____
_____
_____
_____
_____
_____

WRITE ABOUT AN AMERICAN HERO IN YOUR LIFE!

_____
_____
_____
_____
_____
_____

Early Reader Tips
From Dalmatian Press

The **DALMATIAN PRESS EARLY READER SERIES** offers a perfect opportunity to teach children ages 6 through 10 to explore the wonderful world of reading. To inspire you, here are some great tips from Dalmatian Press, a publisher devoted to enriching the lives of children and their families through the magical experience of books. A lifelong love of reading awaits you!

MAKE READING A PART OF EVERY DAY:
* Let children help you choose their books.
* If reading time gives way to other activities, now is the time to restore its proper place in your child's life. As you schedule activities, be sure to include time to find books at the library or from your local store where books are sold.
* When you set bedtimes, build in time for reading.
* Studies agree that reading aloud is the single most important thing a child can do to better succeed in school. Books from Dalmatian Press offer the excitement, character development, and vocabulary that make reading aloud fun.

REASSURE CHILDREN:
* As children grow up, they often find new activities difficult or intimidating. Reassure them by reading about characters who share similar experiences from the **DALMATIAN PRESS EARLY READER SERIES** .

MAKE IT SPECIAL:
* Have a special place where children can keep their books.
* Talk with children about what they are reading. This sends the message that you think reading is important and gives children the chance to reflect on what they've been reading.
* Finally, **have fun** with reading – today and every day!